Nehemiah

God's Builder

A Bible-Based Study

For Individual And Group Use

Leader's Guide included

Lamplighters International
Eden Prairie, Minnesota, USA 55344
www.LamplightersUSA.org

Third printing - October, 2003

Lamplighters International
Eden Prairie, Minnesota USA 55344

Lamplighters International is a Christian ministry that publishes Bible-based, Christ-centered resources.

For additional information about the Lamplighters ministry resources contact:
Lamplighters International P. O. Box 44725, Eden Prairie, Minnesota USA 55344 or visit our web site at www.LamplightersUSA.org.

ISBN # 1-931372-11-x
Order # Ne-NK-SS

Contents

How To Use This Manual

What is Lamplighters™?

Lamplighters is a Christ-centered ministry that is designed to increase your understanding of God's Word and equip you to serve Him more effectively. The ministry consists of a growing series of inductive Bible studies and leadership resources.

A Lamplighters Bible study can be completed as an individual self-study or as part of a Bible study group. Each study is a self-contained unit and an integral part of the entire Lamplighters discipleship ministry.

This Lamplighters study is comprised of seven or fourteen individual lessons, depending on the format you use. When you have completed the entire study you will have earned several new truths and gained a much greater understanding of a significant portion of God's Word.

How To Study A Lamplighters Lesson.

A Lamplighters study begins with your Bible, the weekly lesson, and a sincere desire to learn more about God's Word. The questions are presented in a progressive sequence as you work through the study material. You should not use biblical commentaries or other biblical reference books until you have completed your weekly lesson and met with your weekly group. When you approach the Bible study in this way, you will have the opportunity to discover many valuable spiritual truths from the word of God.

As you prepare for your weekly study, find a quiet place to complete your weekly lesson. You will need approximately one hour to complete each lesson. If you are new to Lamplighters, plan to spend more time on the first few lessons. Your weekly personal study time will decrease as you become familiar with the format. You will look forward each week to discovering important life principles in the coming lessons.

Each lesson is divided into two parts. While some people complete their weekly lesson at one time, others have found it beneficial to complete the studies at two different occasions. If you approach your study time in this way you will be able to reflect more fully upon the difficult biblical passages. If you are meeting as a study group, the Group Leader or Pastor should be available to help you find the answers to any questions you have difficulty with. In addition, many people have found it helpful to begin their study early in the week so that they have enough time to meditate on the questions that require careful consideration.

Your answers should be written in your own words in the space provided on the weekly studies. We have intentionally provided a significant amount of writing space for this purpose. Write down your carefully worded and thoughtful answers with appropriate verse references unless the question calls for a personal opinion. The answers to the questions will be found in the Scripture references at the end of the questions or in the passages listed at the beginning of each study.

How To Use This Discipleship Guide.

The Lamplighters discipleship materials are designed for a variety of ministry applications. They have been used successfully in the following settings:

Self-study - Read the passage carefully that is listed at the beginning of the weekly lesson. Seek to gain as much understanding of the Text as possible. Answer the questions in the space provided using complete sentences if the space allows. Complete the entire lesson without looking at the Leader's Guide in the back of the book. Discipline yourself to answer all the questions so that you gain the maximum benefit from the lesson. When you have completed the lesson, read the corresponding portion of the Leader's Guide to gain greater understanding of the passage you have studied.

One-on-one discipleship – Complete the entire lesson without referring to the Leader's Guide. If you are leading the one-on-one discipleship meeting, become familiar with the Leader's Guide answers before you meet with the person you are discipling. Plan to meet for one hour to discuss the lesson. If you are not leading the study, do not look at the Leader's Guide until you have met with the person who is leading the meeting.

Small Group discipleship - The members of the discipleship group should complete their entire weekly lessons without referring to the Leader's Guide. The Group Leader should complete his or her lesson and then become thoroughly familiar with the Leader's Guide answers. A comprehensive ministry manual has been prepared for church leaders to help them how to lead small groups effectively and how to implement the Lamplighters discipleship ministry into their church ministries.

Class teaching - The teacher should complete the entire lesson before class, review the Leader's Guide answers, and prayerfully consider how to present the lesson. The class members should complete the weekly lessons in advance so that they can bring their thoughtful insights and questions to the class discussion. The Teacher's Edition allows churches to reproduce the Lamplighters Bible Studies for classes within the church. Check out our website for more information on this and other teaching and discipleship resources.

"*Do you think*" Questions

Each weekly study has a few "*do you think*" questions. These questions ask you to make personal applications from the Biblical truths you are learning. Make a special effort to answer these questions because they are designed to help you apply God's Word to your life. In the first lesson the *"do you think"* questions are placed in italic print for easy identification. If you are part of a study group, your insightful answers to these questions could be a great source of spiritual encouragement to others.

Personal Questions

Occasionally you will be asked to respond to personal questions that you should do your best to answer. If you are part of a study group, you will not be asked to share any personal information about yourself. However, be sure to answer these questions for your own benefit because they will help you compare your present level of spiritual maturity to the Biblical principles presented in the lesson.

A Final Word

Throughout this study, the masculine pronouns are often used in the generic sense to avoid awkward sentence construction. When the pronouns "he", "him", "his" are used to refer to the Trinity (God the father, Jesus Christ and the Holy Spirit), they always refer to the masculine gender.

This Lamplighters study is presented after many hours of careful preparation. It is our prayer that it will help you *"... grow in the grace and knowledge of our Lord and Savior Jesus Christ. To Him be the glory, both now and forever. Amen."* (2 Pet. 3:18).

About the author ...

John Stewart was born and raised near Winnipeg, Canada. He was drafted by the Pittsburgh Penguins (NHL) and played professional hockey for eight years. He was born again in 1977 and graduated from seminary in 1988. He has served as a pastor for fifteen years and planted two Bible-believing churches. He founded Lamplighters International where he serves as its president and continues to write and oversee the ministry.

Nehemiah

Introduction

The great missionary William Carey said, *"Attempt great things for God, expect great things from God"*. The book of Nehemiah is a record of how God used a man who dared to trust Him. Nehemiah left the security of a high-ranking government position in Persia to seek the relief of his fellow Jews who were living in Judah. His mission was simple - to provide security for the people of Jerusalem by rebuilding the ancient wall surrounding the city. He accomplished this great work for the people of Jerusalem over two millenniums ago and his testimony has lived on as an inspiration to believers throughout the ages.

Historical Background

In 586 BC, Nebuchadnezzar and his Babylonian army sacked and burned Jerusalem, bringing an end to the southern kingdom of Judah and their formal occupation of Palestine. Many of the Jewish people were taken captive to Babylon as the prophets Isaiah and Jeremiah had prophesied many years earlier. The Babylonians allowed the Jews to build homes and soon many of them became content in their new environment.

In 539 BC, Babylonia was conquered by the Persians who were led by Cyrus the Great. During the first year of his reign (538 BC) Cyrus issued a royal decree allowing the Jewish exiles to return to Palestine (cf. Ezra 1:1-4) so they could rebuild the temple and reestablish the sacrificial system. The first Jewish exiles, led by Zerubbabel (cf. Ezra 1:1-2:70), reconstructed the altar and laid the foundation of the temple (Ezra 3:1-13). Their enemies wrote a letter to King Artaxerxes of Persia accusing the Jews of rebuilding the city so that they could rebel against Persian rule (Ezra 4:11-16). King Artaxerxes of Persia issued a royal decree that stopped the work until the second year of King Darius of Persia (Ezra 4:24).

The Lord raised up two prophets, Haggai and Zechariah, to motivate the Jews to complete the work that Cyrus had originally commissioned them to do (Ezra 5:1). In 458 BC, the scribe Ezra led a second group of exiles to Jerusalem (cf. Ezra 7:1 ff.) and found the temple was still not completed and many of the Jews had intermarried with the pagan people of the land. Ezra oversaw the completion of the temple and led the people to renounce their pagan ways.

Nehemiah led the third and final group of exiles back to Palestine in 445/444 BC - ninety-four years after Cyrus's original decree. As the new governor of Judah, he had authority over all aspects of Jewish life. During his twelve-year stay in Jerusalem. Nehemiah succeeded in rebuilding the wall that surrounded Jerusalem and instituted social and religious reforms among the people.

Purpose and Importance

The book of Nehemiah is a natural sequel to the book of Ezra. In fact, the two Books have always been united in the Jewish Scriptures. The book of Nehemiah provides the second and final part of the historical record of the Jews' return to Palestine. The second purpose for Nehemiah's inclusion in the Bible may be to show how God will use someone who is willing to give up his earthly security and trust Him. Nehemiah was neither a priest nor a prophet, but God used him to accomplish a great work. A third purpose of the book of Nehemiah may be to remind God's people that true spirituality is not the result of proximity to a place of worship. The pre-exilic Jews looked to the temple in Jerusalem with great pride but many of them did not revere God and His laws. God allowed them to be sent into exile in Babylon so that they might understand the error of their ways. The exiled Jews, living first in Babylon and then in Persia, were removed from the temple and longed to return to their homeland and the temple. However, when they had an opportunity to return, many of them chose to remain in exile. Those who returned under Zerubbabel and Ezra soon fell into apostasy. Many years later Jesus told the Samaritan woman at the well words that applied to the Jews who returned from Babylon, *"the hour is coming when you will neither on this mountain, nor in Jerusalem, worship the Father. But the hour is coming, and now is, when the true worshippers will worship the Father in spirit and truth ..."* (Jn. 4:21, 23). A fourth purpose may be to reveal the level of dedication that is necessary to accomplish great things for God. Nehemiah's opposition came from enemies on both sides of the wall and his perseverance is a testimony to God's faithfulness and his own determination.

Study # 1a   **The Priority Of Prayer**

Read - Introduction, Neh. 1:1-2:8; other references as given.

Introduction

1. Which great Christian missionary said, *"Attempt great things for God, expect great things from God"*?

2. Who was Nehemiah (Introduction, cf. Neh. 1:1, 11, 2:1)?

3. What were the original political circumstances that brought the Jews to Babylon?

4. Which Persian king issued the original decree to allow the Jews to return to Palestine?

5. a. After Zerubbabel had led the first Jewish exiles back to Jerusalem, the Jews set up the altar and laid the foundation of the temple. Why weren't they able to complete the temple as they had planned?

    b. The scribe Ezra led the second group of Jewish exiles back to Palestine. What specific things was he able to accomplish after his arrival?

6. King Artaxerxes made Nehemiah the official governor of Judah, which gave him authority over all aspects of Jewish life during his twelve-year stay in Palestine.

    a. When did Nehemiah first arrive in Jerusalem?

    b. What important things was he able to accomplish during this time?

7. The book of Nehemiah is an important part of God's revelation to man. List four purposes or themes for the book of Nehemiah.

Part b - Neh. 1:1-2:10

8. In the twentieth year of King Artaxerxes (i.e., 445 BC), during the month of Chislev (i.e., Nov.-Dec.), Nehemiah was visited at Sushan by his brother Hanani and some other men who had recently returned from Jerusalem. Sushan was the winter capital of the Persian kings, located about 150 miles north of the Persian Gulf.

    a. During Hanani's visit, what two questions did Nehemiah ask him (Neh. 1:2)?

    b. What was Hanani's reply (Neh. 1:3)?

9. At first glance Nehemiah's reaction to Hanani's report seems extreme (v. 4). However, ancient Jews often threw dust on their heads, tore their clothes, fasted, and sat on low stools during times of mourning or grief (cf. Job 1:20; Ps. 137:1; Es. 4:16). Why was Nehemiah so distressed when he heard Hanani's report (Neh. 2:3)?

10. Great leaders are not just men and women who possess superior leadership abilities. They are often individuals who allow their hearts to be stirred with the needs of others and attempt to meet these needs.

    a. Give the names of three other individuals who were also moved with compassion and give a brief statement how each one attempted to meet the needs they saw (Matt. 14:13-19; Acts 17:16, 17; Phil. 2:25-30).

    b. All around us are people in great distress (sickness and death, job layoff or financial problems, divorce and family conflict, the plight of the unborn, etc.). Please list several practical ways *you think* God's people can be used to meet these needs?

11. Nehemiah was so grieved for people he had never met that he forsook his comfortable position in the Persian court and moved to Palestine. He endangered his life to build a wall around the city of Jerusalem that would help protect the people. What are you (and your family) currently doing to help others in need?

12. Nehemiah knew that he was facing a problem that was beyond his ability to overcome. Rather than becoming overwhelmed by despair, he turned to God in prayer (Neh. 1:5-11). Many Christians have been taught the acronym ACTS (adoration, confession, thanksgiving, supplication) as a reminder of the key elements of prayer. Examine Nehemiah's prayer and list as many of the four elements of prayer as you can find and give a phrase (including verse ref.) to support your view (Neh. 1:5-11).

13. Power in prayer comes from an individual's relationship to God, his willingness to humble himself before God, and knowing how to pray according to His will. A believer's humility (or lack thereof) is often manifested in the words that he prays.

   a. In Nehemiah's prayer, he uses a two-word phrase seven times that indicates his willingness to humble himself before God. What is it (Neh. 1:5-11)?

   b. Many Christians' prayers could be described as "give-me prayers". Rather than acknowledging God's magnificence and the believer's responsibility to submit to Him as Nehemiah did, their prayers are often a grocery list of requests. Take a moment to reflect on your prayers to God. Do you regularly praise His holy name and confess your sins to Him when you pray?

14. Sometimes believers fail to receive answers to their prayers because they ask God for only general blessings (e.g., God, please bless all the people all the time forever and ever. Amen.). In Nehemiah's prayer, what specific requests did he ask God to grant him (Neh. 1:8-11)?

15. Sometime after Nehemiah began to pray and fast (Nisan =March-April), King Artaxerxes noticed Nehemiah's sadness of heart (Neh. 2:2). Ancient Persian art from Persepolis indicates that those who came into the king's presence were to show the greatest respect, even placing the right hand over their mouth so as not to defile the king with their breath. Nehemiah, recognizing that the king could take his life, fearfully explained the source of his anguish to the king.

    a. What did Nehemiah do when King Artaxerxes said, **"What do you request?"** (Neh. 2:4, 5)?

    b. In what way(s) do you normally respond when you are afraid?

    c. Fear is such a terrible, controlling emotion that some people will use almost any human remedy to alleviate their anxiety. What is God's cure for fear (1 Jn. 4:18)?

16. How did Nehemiah show sensitivity to the king and the needs of the royal court when the king asked him, **"How long will your journey be? And when will you return?"** (Neh. 2:6)?

17. a.   When King Artaxerxes gave Nehemiah permission to return to Jerusalem (v. 6), Nehemiah took the opportunity to make two bold requests of the king. What were they (Neh. 2:7, 8)?

    b.   Nehemiah asked the king for an extended leave of absence, official letters of endorsement, and timber for construction of the walls. What *do you think* his request for all these things signifies?

Psalm 119:105 "Your word is a lamp to my feet and a light to my path."

Study # 2a   **The Power Of A Clear Vision**

Read - Neh. 2:9-4:23; other references as given.

1. Nehemiah was accompanied by several Persian officers and horsemen during his journey to Jerusalem (Neh. 2:9). Bible scholars estimate this journey took approximately two to three months (Note: Ezra's return, 14 years earlier, took four months with a much larger group, cf. Ezra 7:8, 9). No doubt Nehemiah was excited to arrive safely at Jerusalem (Neh. 2:11). What was the first response to Nehemiah's arrival (Neh. 2:10)?

2. Nehemiah likely spent the first three days in Jerusalem recuperating from the long and strenuous journey (v. 11, cf. Ezra 8:32). After three days, Nehemiah arose in the night to inspect the wall (vv.12-16; note: it was probably the first moonlit night). He told no one what God had directed him to do for Jerusalem (v. 12).

    a. Why do you think he was so secretive about his activities during this time (vv. 12-17)?

    b. From the time of Nehemiah's arrival, to the completion of his inspection of the wall, his actions reveal several important principles about effective leadership. Please list at least three (Neh. 2:10-16).

3. After Nehemiah had completed a thorough inspection of the southern portion of the wall (i.e., the Valley Gate, the Dragon's Well, etc.), he called all the people together and communicated his vision to them (Neh. 2:17, 18). List at least three things Nehemiah said to the Jews that would have encouraged them to enthusiastically support the rebuilding of the wall (Neh. 2:17, 18)?

4. Nehemiah said **Come and let us build the wall of Jerusalem, that we may no longer be a reproach** (Neh. 2:17). The clarity of Nehemiah's challenge presented the Jews with a clear objective - to work together to rebuild the wall. Occasionally leaders (pastors, ministry leaders, employers, parents, etc.) become frustrated with their people even though they have never communicated clearly defined expectations. Are you certain that those who are looking to you for leadership know what you expect of them (e.g., fellow workers, children, etc.)?   If you are uncertain, ask them to tell you what they think you expect of them.

5. Another important characteristic of godly leadership is the ability to handle criticism effectively. It would have been easy for Nehemiah to react negatively to Sanballat, Tobiah and Geshem's attack on his motives. Nehemiah used it as an opportunity to testify for God when he said, **The God of heaven Himself will prosper us** (Neh. 2:20).

    a. Nehemiah's enemies attacked two specific areas of his leadership (Neh. 2:19). Examine their two questions and try to identify the specific areas of attack that every leader might experience (Neh. 2:19).

    b. How is the Lord's bondservant supposed to respond when someone falsely accuses or wrongs him (2 Tim. 2:24, 25)?

6. When believers react defensively toward the criticism of others, they reject an important means that God uses to impart spiritual truth. Rather than making it easy for others to point out weaknesses and faults, the individual's defensive nature (cf. Gen. 3:8-13) hinders his spiritual progress by setting up an emotional defense system that keeps others away.

    a. Do you regularly react negatively (e.g., justify your actions, attack other people, pout, etc.) when someone points out something you have done wrong?

    b. What specific things could you do to become more receptive to the criticism of others?

7. Nehemiah's record of the initial reconstruction of the wall (Neh. 3:1-32) is probably a summary of the notable individuals and families who contributed to the work. His summary of the work begins on the northeast side of the wall and proceeds counterclockwise. Many Christians do not apply themselves to a diligent study of certain passages such as this because they do not believe there is much spiritual benefit to be gained. What important truth should God's people remember when they study a portion of Scripture such as this one (2 Tim. 3:16, 17)?

8. Reconstruction of various portions of the wall was assigned to specific groups and families. The wall had lain in ruins since its destruction by Nebuchadnezzar about 130 years earlier. Why do you think Eliashib, the high priest, is mentioned first, and why was he assigned to rebuild the Sheep Gate (Neh. 3:1)?

Study # 2b   The Power Of A Clear Vision

9.   Nehemiah's plan was to work on all portions of the wall (including the gates) simultaneously rather than completing one section of the wall at a time (cf. Neh. 4:6). In several instances, the workers worked on the wall directly in front of their own homes (cf. Neh. 3:10, 23, 29, 30).

   a.   What would be some of the specific benefits of approaching the work in this manner?

   b.   How could this leadership principle be applied in your home, church, or place of employment?

10.   Nehemiah's frequent use of the phrase **next to** (used 15 X's) seems to emphasize the effective coordination of the work (Neh. 3:1-32). What specific benefit(s) do you think would have been accomplished by having the builders work so closely to each other?

11.   Nehemiah makes special note that the Tekoite nobles (Heb. *addirim* - exalted one, majestic ones, i.e., aristocrats) did not support the work (Neh. 3:5).

   a.   What was Nehemiah's response to their unwillingness to work on the wall (Neh. 3:5)?

b.   When someone fails to fulfill his responsibility in a cooperative work effort, there is a possibility that the job will not be completed as planned. When this happens, the Lord often inspires someone to go the "extra mile" and fulfill the need. There is one group who repaired more than one section of the wall. Who was it (Neh. 3:27)?

12. Every time a believer or a church attempts to accomplish a great work of God, they can expect resistance from the enemies of God. As the building of the wall continued, the enemies of God intensified their efforts to thwart the rebuilding of the wall (Neh. 4:1-3). During Nehemiah's first encounter with his enemies, they attempted to hinder the work by questioning the wisdom of his plan and his motives (cf. Neh. 2:19).

a.   In addition to repeating their original attack on his wisdom and his motives, what did Tobiah do to hurt the work (Neh. 4:3)?

b.   How did Nehemiah react to Tobiah's attempt to stop the work (Neh. 4:5, 6)?

13. As the work of God increases, so does the resistance of God's enemies upon His people (cf. Neh. 4:7, 8). When Nehemiah became aware that His enemies were conspiring to attack the city and stop the work, he called the people together for prayer and set up a guard (Neh. 4:9).

a.   Do you think the setting up of a guard was a lack of faith?   Why?

b. What does this verse teach about the relationship between trusting God in prayer and the believer's personal responsibility?

14. The laborious work of rebuilding the wall and the threat of enemy attack took its toll on the builders (Neh. 4:10). How did Nehemiah protect himself and the people from the threat of discouragement and the threat of a surprise enemy attack (Neh. 4:10-14)?

15. Nehemiah's enemies attempted to intimidate him with the threat of a surprise attack (Neh. 4:11, 12). He used this information to motivate his workers to prepare for enemy attack. Although Nehemiah could have taken credit for this situation to bolster the people's confidence in his leadership, he refused to profit from the turn of events.

a. Who did Nehemiah credit for overcoming this crisis (Neh. 4:15)?

b. How did the people respond to his godly leadership after the crisis had passed (Neh. 4:15)?

16. How did Nehemiah protect the people and the work from the ongoing threat of enemy attack (Neh. 4:16-23)?

17. Some of the builders carried weapons in one hand and worked with the other. Others stood guard with shields, spears, bows, and breastplates (Neh. 4:16). How can Christians protect themselves and others from the attacks of Satan (Eph. 6:10-18)?

Psalm 119:105 *"Your word is a lamp to my feet and a light to my path."*

Study # 3a   How To Overcome Adversity

Read - Neh. 5:1-6:19; other references as given.

1.   A great leader must possess the ability to overcome adversity. Nehemiah overcame the attacks of Sanballat, Tobiah and Geshem by turning to God in prayer and refusing to become sidetracked from the work. In chapter six, Nehemiah faced a new challenge - internal conflict among the people.

   a.   There were two groups of people in Jerusalem who were at odds with each other. Who were they (Neh. 5:1-5, 7)?

   b.   The people and their wives had three specific problems with their Jewish brothers (Neh. 5:2-5). What were they?

2.   a.   What was Nehemiah's immediate emotional reaction to this social injustice (Neh. 5:6)?

   b.   Rather than exploding in anger, Nehemiah gave **... serious thought** (Neh. 5:7). What do you think this means?

3.   What is your normal response when something or someone makes you angry? Do you take some time to give serious thought to situations before you do something rash or hasty?

4. Some people fail to resolve problems that really need to be addressed. Rather than addressing the problem in a Christ-like manner, they ignore the problem hoping their negative feelings will disappear. Nehemiah did four things that resulted in an effective resolution of the problem. What were they (Neh. 5:7-12)?

5. What had the Jewish nobles and the rulers done wrong (Neh. 5:8; cf. Ex. 22:25; Lev. 25:39-43; De. 23:19)?

6. When the greedy Jewish nobles and rulers were confronted by Nehemiah they acknowledged their sin.

   a. What two things did Nehemiah want them to do (Neh. 5:10, 11)?

   b. Unfortunately, some Christians believe that a sincere apology is all that is necessary when they sin. While sincere confession is important, God's people should make restitution if possible to the one who was wronged. Give the names of two individuals who demonstrated the sincerity of their repentance by a willingness to make restitution (Lu. 19:1-8, Philemon 8-16).

   c. Is there someone of whom you should seek forgiveness and make restitution?

7. Another quality of a godly leader is his unwillingness to take advantage of his position. Nehemiah was a godly servant who saw himself as an example for the people to follow rather than an exception who could take advantage of every financial opportunity.

    a. In what way(s) did Nehemiah demonstrate a sacrificial servant's heart during his twelve-year reign as governor of Judah (Neh. 5:14-18)?

    b. Nehemiah's personal sacrifice of not using the governor's food allowance stands in stark contrast to the Jewish nobles' action of taking advantage of the poor. Why did Nehemiah not use his food allowance (Neh. 5:15-18)?

8. Every Christian should strive to be a good witness for Christ by willingly sacrificing for others around them. What sacrifices do you regularly make for others (your family, fellow Christians, fellow employees, etc.) because of your fear and reverence for God?

9. When Sanballat and his friends heard that the wall had been completed except for the doors on the gates, they tried to lure Nehemiah out of Jerusalem (Neh. 6:2-4). They wanted him to meet them in the plain of Ono (Note: the plain of Ono is located seven miles southeast of Joppa). What reason did Nehemiah give for not meeting with them (Neh. 6:3)?

Study # 3b   How To Overcome Adversity

10. Nehemiah was not a priest who taught the Law or a mighty prophet who spoke God's Word to the people. He was a former government official who repaired a wall around an ancient city. God used him in a great way because he believed God had given him a great work to do. Many Christians struggle with a sense of spiritual unworthiness, believing that God has overlooked them for significant spiritual service. Take a minute to seriously evaluate your life and service before God. Do you consider your service to God (as an employee, a father or mother, your ministry through your local church) as a great work for God?   Why?

11. Nehemiah's enemies sent four messages for him to meet with them but he refused to meet each time (Neh. 6:4). Finally, Sanballat sent his servant with an open letter (Neh. 6:5). An ancient official letter was ordinarily written on papyrus or a leather sheet, rolled up, tied with a string, and sealed with a hardened clay impression called a bulla to guarantee its authenticity and privacy. Why do you think Sanballat sent his letter unsealed?

12. Sanballat's slanderous letter to Nehemiah is a classic example of the things gossips and slanderers often say and do when they spread their poison (Neh. 6:6, 7).

    a. Examine Sanballat's letter carefully. What three things did Sanballat say in his open letter that are characteristic of the things that other gossips and slanderers say (Neh. 6:6, 7).

    b. Gossip and slander are powerful weapons that Satan has used to attack the work of God. How powerful is slander (Pro. 16:28)?

c.   How does the Bible describe a person who slanders (Pro. 10:18)?

13. Gossip and slander are wicked acts of cowardly revenge that God's people should not use. What two things did Nehemiah do when Sanballat slanderously attacked him (Neh. 6:8, 9)?

14. Sanballat and Tobiah hired false prophets who tried to frighten Nehemiah (Neh. 6:10-14). A false prophet named Shemaiah encouraged Nehemiah to flee into the temple building, but Nehemiah **perceived that God had not sent him at all** (Neh. 6:12).

a.   How did Nehemiah know that his prophecy was false (Nu. 18:7; cf. Lev. 21:17-24)?

b.   Why did Nehemiah's enemies want him to flee into the temple building (Neh. 6:13)?

c.   What did Nehemiah do to strengthen himself during this last attack from his enemies (Neh. 6:14)?

15. Nehemiah trusted God, overcame all obstacles, and did not allow himself to become distracted from his work. Amazingly the wall of Jerusalem that had lain in ruins for approximately 130 years was rebuilt in only fifty-two days (Neh. 6:15). What two things happened to Nehemiah's enemies when they heard that the wall had been completed (Neh. 6:16)?

16. Tobiah was doubly related to influential families in Judah. He was the son-in-law of Shechaniah (apparently an influential man in Judah) and his son was married to the daughter of Meshullam (Note: Meshullam made repairs on the wall; cf. Neh. 3:4, 30).

    a. What problems did this cause Nehemiah (Neh. 6:17-19)?

    b. From what you know already about Nehemiah's character, what do you think he did when he heard his fellow Jews telling him about Tobiah's good deeds (Neh. 6:19)?

17. What were the most significant lessons taught in this lesson?

Psalm 119:105 "Your word is a lamp to my feet and a light to my path."

Study # 4a   One Nation Under God

Read - Neh. 7:1-8:18; other references as given.

1.   What did Nehemiah do after the wall was completed (Neh. 7:1, 2)?

2.   The Text says Nehemiah appointed his brother Hanani and a man named Hananiah as joint administrators over Jerusalem. The striking similarity between these two names has led some interpreters to believe that the two names refer to the same person (Note: the original Hebrew language allows for this possible interpretation).

    a.   How can we be sure that Nehemiah appointed two men, Hanani and Hananiah, to oversee Jerusalem (Neh. 7:1-3; cf. Neh. 3:8, 12)?

    b.   What two qualities did Hananiah possess that made him a wise choice to help oversee Jerusalem (Neh. 7:2)?

3.   One of God's primary characteristics is His immutability that means that He does not change (cf. Mal. 3:6; Heb. 13:8). Because God is immutable, He is faithful and believers can trust Him implicitly to act according to His Word (cf. Heb. 10:23). God has given Christians three precious promises that are specifically guaranteed by His faithfulness.

    a.   What are they (1 Cor. 10:13; 2 Thess. 3:3; 1 Jn. 1:9)?

b.   Faithfulness is an essential quality of an effective Christian servant (cf. 1 Cor. 4:2; 2 Tim. 2:2). What do you think it means for a Christian to be faithful?

c.   Are you faithful to God? ...your family? ...your friends? ...your church?

4.   Some Christians believe that they would become more faithful if they were given greater responsibility in life (e.g., a job promotion, a new church ministry, etc.). However, the Bible teaches that God's people must learn to be faithful to their present responsibilities if they want to be given more responsibility in the future (cf. Lu. 16:10).

a.   What did the good and faithful slave receive for his responsible service to his master (Matt. 25:19-21)?

b.   What can God's people expect if they are not faithful stewards of the financial resources that God has entrusted to their administration (Lu. 16:10, 11)? Note: mammon is a word of Aramaic origin that means riches, treasure.

c.   What do you think are the **true riches** (Lu. 16:11-13)?

5.   Nehemiah ordered the people not to open the city gates until the sun was hot, to protect the city from the threat of surprise enemy attack (Note: the gate would normally be opened at sunrise). He also commanded the guards to shut and bolt the doors before they went off duty at night (Neh. 7:3). Next, he planned to take a census of the people living in Palestine (Neh. 7:5). Why did Nehemiah plan to take a census (Neh. 7:4, 5)?

6. Nehemiah found a genealogical record of the original exiles who had returned to Jerusalem under Zerubbabel (Neh. 7:8-62). Although the list is strikingly similar to the list recorded in Ezra 2:3-70, there are some notable differences (Note: Nehemiah's list has 1,271 more returning exiles).

    a. What do you think could account for these different totals?

    b. Why were some of the priests excluded from the priesthood (Neh. 7:63, 64; cf. Lev. 21:14, 15)?

7. When the wall had been built and the necessary administrative duties had been assigned, the Jewish people gathered together in front of the water gate (Neh. 8:1). They gathered on the first day of the seventh month that was the beginning of the civil calendar (Note: the seventh month, Tishri, corresponds to Sept. - Oct.). The priest, Ezra, who had returned from exile in 458 BC 14 years before Nehemiah, was asked to address the people (Neh. 8:1).

    a. Ezra addressed the men, women, and all who could understand, from early morning to midday (Neh. 8:2,3). What was the content of Ezra's message to the Jewish people (Neh. 8:1-3)?

    b. The Jewish people had three notable responses to the reading of the book of the Law. What were they (Neh. 8:3, 5, 9)?

8. Unfortunately, many Christians have a low view of the authority of God's Word. While they give mental assent to the doctrine of Biblical inspiration, they tend to view the Word of God as an option to be considered rather than an imperative to be obeyed. What are some evidences that a believer has a low view of God's Word even though he believes the Bible is the inspired Word of God?

9. If an individual believer or a local church submits to the authority of God's Word, their lives will be changed and God will use them in a mighty way for His glory.

    a. For what did the apostle Paul commend the Thessalonian church (1 Thess. 2:13)?

    b. How had their lives changed (1 Thess. 1:6-10)?

    c. What did Paul say about the Thessalonian believers' witness for Christ (1 Thess. 1:8)?

10. It is likely that Ezra and the thirteen other men stood on a specially prepared wooden platform (Heb. *Migdal* - tower) overlooking the people (Neh. 8:4). Some interpreters have suggested that Ezra and the others read successive portions of the Law of Moses. At selected intervals, the men mentioned in verse seven and the Levites, would mingle among the people and explain the Law to them (Neh. 8:6, 7). Many Bible teachers believe that Ezra's method of communicating God's Word (i.e., reading a selected portion of the Text and explaining it) is the acceptable Biblical pattern that all preachers and Bible teachers should follow. Do you agree?   Why?

11. What did the apostle Paul tell Timothy to emphasize in his public ministry to the church at Ephesus (2 Tim. 4:1-3)?   Why (vv. 3, 4)?

12. Some religious leaders seem to teach everything but the Word of God. What are some things that unprincipled men teach rather than God's Word (Mk. 7:5-9; 1 Tim. 1:3-7)?

13. Why is it so important for God's servants (pastors, missionaries, Sunday School teachers, etc.) to teach the Word of God to their hearers (Ro. 10:17; 2 Tim. 3:16, 17; Heb. 4:12)?

14. On the second day of the gathering, Ezra spoke to the heads of the Jewish families (i.e., clans), priests, and Levites so that they could gain greater insight into the words of the Law (Neh. 8:13).

    a. What did they learn from Ezra's teaching (Neh. 8:14)?

    b. How did they respond to their new understanding of the will of God (Neh. 8:15-17)?

    c. What emotional response did they experience as a result of their obedience (v. 17)?

15. It is interesting that the heads of the families joined the priests and the Levites to gain greater understanding of the Law of God. In a day when many fathers have abdicated their spiritual responsibilities to their families, this example (i.e., the Jewish fathers) serves as a powerful example of the need for male spiritual leadership within the home.

    a. What Biblical responsibility has God given every Christian father (Eph. 6:4)?

    b. What spiritual advice would you give a young Christian father who desired to fulfill this important spiritual responsibility?

Psalm 119:105 "Your word is a lamp to my feet and a light to my path."

Study # 5a Getting Right With God

1. The Feast of Tabernacles (booths) concluded on the 22nd day of the month. After a one day interval, the people assembled again on the 24th of the month (Neh. 9:1). This time, they gathered to hear Ezra read the Law of Moses and to confess their sins. The Word of God had had a tremendous impact on the Jewish community by pointing out their sin (Neh. 8:9), leading them to worship (Neh. 8:12, 14) and giving them joy (Neh. 8:17). How did the Jews demonstrate the genuineness of their repentance (Neh. 9:1, 2)?

2. Many Christians are not aware of the true nature of Biblical repentance. The Bible teaches that Pharaoh of Egypt repented but his repentance was insincere because he returned to his sin when the threat of punishment was removed (cf. Ex. 9:27-34). The Bible teaches that Judas Iscariot repented but his repentance was also insincere because he did not turn to God (cf. Matt. 27:3-5). Years later, the apostle Paul wrote to the Corinthians, commending them for the sincerity of their repentance.

    a. Please list the characteristics of genuine repentance (2 Cor. 7:9-11)?

    b. In what way(s) do you think a knowledge of the characteristics of genuine repentance might help Christian parents raise their children to be godly?

3.   Interestingly, the ninth chapters of Ezra, Nehemiah, and Daniel are all devoted to the confession of national sin and prayer for God's mercy and grace. Why do you think the Jews separated themselves from all the foreigners (Neh. 9:2)?

4.   Eight Levites led the people in prayer (Neh. 9: 4, 5). They praised God for who He is (vv. 5-8), reviewed His goodness and their sin since the time of the exodus (vv. 9-31), acknowledged that their present distress (i.e., slavery) was a direct result of their failure (vv. 32-37), and committed themselves to walk in God's ways (v. 38; cf. Neh. 10:28-30). In the phrase, **Your glorious name,** the word **glory** (Heb. *kabod*) comes from a root word that means "weighty".

     a.   In what way(s) do you think God's name is weighty (Neh. 9:5)?

     b.   Why is Abraham specifically mentioned in this first part of the Levites' prayer (Neh. 9:7, 8; Gen. 12:1-3, 15:18-21, 17:1-5)?

5.   a.   For what did the Levites praise God as they led the people in prayer (Neh. 9:6-9)?

     b.   When you pray, do you regularly praise God for these things?

6.   Nehemiah 9:9-31 is a historic overview of God's faithfulness to Israel from the nation's beginning to the time of the Assyrian and Babylonian captivities. It is also a review of Israel's unfaithfulness to God during the same period.

a. What did God do for Abraham's descendants (i.e., the Jews) in response to their cry for help (Neh. 9:9-11)?

b. Why did God destroy Pharaoh's army (**their persecutors**, v. 11) when He rescued His people from Egypt (Gen. 12:3)?

7. Next the Levites' prayer addressed Israel's initial journey in the desert and at Mount Sinai (Neh. 9:12-21). God's faithfulness is demonstrated during this time by the wondrous deeds which He performed in their midst (vv. 12-15).

a. God provided divine guidance (v. 12), revealed His Law to them through Moses (vv. 13, 14), and gave them bread (manna) and water (vv. 14, 15). What words or phrases are used to describe God's revelation to man (Neh. 9:13)?

b. How did the ancient Israelites respond to God's ordinances, laws, and commandments that are right and true (Neh. 9:16, 17)?

8. It is very interesting that only one of the commandments, **Remember the Sabbath day, to keep it holy,** is specifically mentioned in the prayer (Neh. 9:14; cf. Ex. 20:8). Unfortunately, some Christians forsake their Biblical responsibility to gather weekly with other believers for spiritual rejuvenation (cf. Heb. 10:25). Believing that Sunday is simply a day of rest, they engage in various non-strenuous work projects and leisure activities that provide very little spiritual renewal. What happens when God's people are unwilling to set aside time each week for spiritual instruction and worship (Neh. 9:16, 17)?

9. How did God respond to the Israelites' rebellion during their wilderness wanderings (Neh. 9:18-21)?

Study # 5b   Getting Right With God

Read - Neh. 9:1-10:39; other references as given.

10. After forty years of wandering in the wilderness, God blessed the Israelites abundantly by allowing them to enter the Promised Land (Neh. 9:22-25).

    a.   What did Moses tell the people to do when they entered the land (De. 8:1, 2, 11-14)?

    b.   What did the Israelites do when they entered the land (Neh. 9:26)?

11. God could have entirely forsaken those who rebelled against Him but He chose to allow neighboring nations to oppress them (Neh. 9:27). Who were the deliverers whom God raised up to rescue his people (Neh. 9:27; Ju. 2:14-16)?

12. What did the Jewish people do when they had been rescued from their oppressors (Neh. 9:28-31)?

13. Finally, the Levites led the people to acknowledge that their present distress (i.e., enslaved to another nation, cf. Neh. 9:32) was a direct result of their failure to obey God (Neh. 9:33-37). The Israelites' understanding of their nation's history (i.e., their own rebellious ways and God's faithfulness to them since the time of the exodus) enabled them to see a dangerous national spiritual pattern. What did they do to prevent this sinful pattern from continuing in the future (Neh. 9:38)?

14. Every individual is the most recent addition to a long and often predictable family history. It has been said that a particular individual paid two hundred dollars to discover his family tree and had to pay another two thousand dollars to cover up the evidence.

   a. Sin patterns can often be traced from one generation to another (cf. Gen. 12:10-19, 26:6-11). How well do you know your family history? Are you knowledgeable of a particular sin pattern that has existed in your family (e.g., anger, lust, covetousness, bitterness, etc.) against which you need to guard?

   b. If you are a parent, what specific spiritual commitments have you made to ensure that the sinful habits of past generations will not be passed on to your children?

15. Several civil and religious leaders joined the heads of many families in signing a covenant to walk in God's ways (Neh. 9:38-10:27). Although the rest of the people did not place their names on the sealed document (Neh. 10:28, 29), they verbally placed themselves under a curse that called upon God to bring down calamity if they failed to fulfill their agreement. The people made several important commitments to God (Neh. 10:30-39). Please list the four spiritual commitments that the people made (Neh. 10:30, 31, 32-34, 35-39).

16. Examine closely each of the spiritual commitments that the people made to help them walk in God's Law (Neh.10:30-39). Using the Jews' commitments as an example, list at least three spiritual commitments you think every Christian should make to help him live according to God's plan.

17. All the Jewish people who **... had knowledge and understanding** (cf. Neh. 10:28) said **... we will not neglect the house of our God** (Neh. 10:39).

    a. What did they mean?

    b. Have you made that same commitment to God?

Psalm 119:105 "Your word is a lamp to my feet and a light to my path."

Study # 6a   Celebrating God's Victories

Read - Neh. 11:1-12:47; other references as given.

1.   God motivated Nehemiah to take a census of the people to determine why so few
     people were living in Jerusalem (cf. Neh. 7:4, 5). When Ezra and the others
     completed the reading of the Law of Moses (cf. Neh. 8:1-18), the people confessed
     their sins and the iniquities of their fathers (Neh. 9:1-37) and made a commitment to
     walk in the ways of the Lord (Neh. 10:1-39). Next, Nehemiah returned to the task of
     repopulating Jerusalem (Neh. 11:1 ff.). How did Nehemiah and the Jews resolve the
     problem of repopulating Jerusalem (Neh. 11:1)?

2.   Throughout Biblical times the casting of the lot was a frequent way of determining
     God's will (cf. Lev. 16:8; Jos. 18:6-10; Matt 27:35; Acts 1:26). Do you think the casting
     of lots is a legitimate way of determining God's will nowadays?   Why?

3.   Many Christians are confused about how to determine God's will for their lives. Their
     confusion leads to a lack of peace (and the inevitable by-product - a loss of joy) and a
     fearful attitude toward serving God.

     a.   How do you currently determine if a specific decision (taking a different job,
          relocation to another state, getting married, making a major purchase, etc.) is
          God's will for your life?

     b.   How can a Christian consistently know God's will for his life (Ro. 12:1, 2)?

4. One tenth of the people living outside of Jerusalem were chosen by lot to move to Jerusalem. It must have been difficult for them to leave their extended families and homes and move to a city that still lay in ruins (cf. Neh. 7:4). However, some people volunteered to move to Jerusalem (Neh. 11:2).

    a. How did the Jewish people respond to those who volunteered to move (Neh. 11:2)?

    b. The spirit of volunteerism is often a great encouragement and challenge to others in the work of the Lord. How do you normally react when you see another Christian volunteering to serve the Lord?

    c. Why do you think volunteerism is often a great encouragement to the work of God?

    d. Do you volunteer at work? ...at home? ...at church?

5. Some of the priests and Levites lived in the Judean towns and villages and traveled to Jerusalem when they served in the temple (Neh. 11:3). The total of the descendants of the various family heads who moved into Jerusalem was 3,044 (468 laymen from the tribe of Judah, vv. 4b-6; 928 laymen from Benjamin, vv. 7-9; 1,192 priests, vv. 10-14; 284 Levites, vv. 15-18; 172 gatekeepers, v. 19). The substantial number of priests who served the Lord and the people indicates the importance of the Old Testament sacrificial system to OT Israel.

    a. What does it also indicate (Heb. 7:23-28, 10:11, 12)?

b. Who was this priest who offered up one sacrifice for sins for all time to whom God said **sit on My right hand til I make Your enemies Your footstool** (Heb. 1:13, cf. Heb. 10:12-14)?

6. The OT priests were required to serve the Lord according to the stipulations of the Mosaic Law. A significant portion of God's Word provides a detailed explanation of the Law that God gave to Moses on Mount Sinai (cf. Ex. 20:1-Nu. 10:10). Besides providing the infant Israelite nation with a national constitution, the Law of Moses reveals the character of God, His moral standard for man, and man's need for forgiveness. For what two reasons was the Law of Moses <u>not</u> given to man (Ro. 3:19, 20; Gal. 4:9-11)? Note: the weak and worthless elemental things are the stipulations of the OT Law.

7. Nehemiah's record of the people who moved to Jerusalem (Neh. 11:4b-19) indicates that some of them served in leadership positions (cf. Neh. 11:9, 11, 16, 17, 21) while others supported the work by their faithful service (Neh. 11:12, 14, 19). The words and phrases that Nehemiah used to identify those who served in a supervisory position provides the excellent mini-profile of an effective leader. Using the following verses, list at least three essential characteristics of an effective leader (Neh. 11:9, 11, 16, 17, 21).

Celebrating God's Victories

8. Some believers are ineffective in their service to God because they are not content to be His servants. They either resist God's plan for leadership, like Moses and Gideon (cf. Ex. 3:7-4:14; Ju. 6:12-15), or they have secret desires for self-advancement, like the Lord's disciples, James and John (cf. Mk. 10:35-37).

   a. Please give four characteristics of an individual who is not content to be a servant of God and one who has secret desires for self-advancement among God's people (3 Jn. 9, 10)?

   b. What specific evidences do you see in your life that you are becoming a more dedicated servant of God?

9. Nehemiah also organized the **singers in charge of the service of the house of God** (Neh. 11:22, 23). Music has always been an important part of man's worship of God (cf. Ex. 15:1-21; Ju. 5:31; Psalms, etc.). Throughout the history of the church, musical expression has been an important but often controversial issue among God's people. What basic principles should govern musical expression among all of God's people (Col. 3:16)?

10. Beginning in chapter twelve, Nehemiah lists the 22 leaders of the priests who had returned from Babylon with Zerubbabel and Jeshua almost 100 years earlier (Neh. 12:1-7). King David had previously appointed 24 priestly divisions to serve in the temple (cf. 1 Chr. 24:7-19) but, apparently, two priestly orders could not be filled (cf. Neh. 7:63-65). Next, the names of several Levites (Neh. 12:8, 9), the generations of high priests and priestly families (Neh. 12:8-21) are listed. What purpose do you think these detailed genealogical lists provide for God's people today?

11. Nehemiah had the Levites from the surrounding towns and villages come to Jerusalem to celebrate the dedication of the wall (Neh. 12:27 ff.). Nehemiah's dedication of the wall of Jerusalem finds precedent in Solomon's dedication of the original temple (2 Chr. 5:13). Like Solomon, Nehemiah made the celebration one of praise and thanksgiving. What did the people do to prepare for the celebration (Neh. 12:27-31)?

12. a. What specific things do you do each Sunday to prepare yourself and your family to celebrate the good things God has done for you and others?

    b. What recommendations would you offer another Christian who wanted to make his corporate worship more meaningful?

13. Two great choirs (companies) of thanksgiving assembled on the top of the western section of the wall and moved in opposite directions (Neh. 12:31, 38; note: The wall was approximately four miles in length). The first choir, led by Ezra (v. 36), moved counterclockwise around the wall. The second choir, of which Nehemiah was part (v. 38), moved clockwise around the wall. The two choirs met at the temple (Neh. 12:40). What happened when all the people assembled at the temple (Neh. 12:40-43)?

14. Many people (including some Christians) make the pursuit of happiness or joy their ultimate goal in life. Even though they spend their entire lives trying to find happiness in the things they possess, the relationships they pursue, and the experiences they encounter, they die without realizing their elusive dream.

   a.   When the people assembled at the temple on the day of dedicating the wall, they experienced such great joy that **the joy of Jerusalem was heard afar off** (Neh. 12:43). What happened that caused them to experience such joy?

   b.   How can a Christian become truly joyful (Neh. 12:43; Jn. 15:11; 17:13)?

   c.   If a Christian is not joyful, it is an indication that his primary objective in life is not to please God. Take a moment to seriously examine your life. Can you honestly say that pleasing God is the ultimate goal in your life?

Psalm 119:105 "Your word is a lamp to my feet and a light to my path."

Study # 7a   **Finishing Your Work**

Read - Neh. 13:1-31; other references as given.

1. On an unspecified day the people gathered again to hear the Law of Moses (Neh. 13:1). What did they discover (Neh. 13:1)?

2. a. The portion of the book of Moses from which the people read was Deuteronomy 23:3-5. What did they do when they learned that **no Ammonite or Moabite should ever come into the assembly of God** (Neh. 13:1-3)?

    b. Why had Moses told the Israelites that neither Ammonites nor Moabites could enter the congregation of God (Neh. 13:1, 2; Nu. 22:1-6)?

3. God's judgment on the Ammonites and Moabites seems rather harsh until we recognize that they were closely related to Israel and had an obligation to help the Israelites.

    a. In what way were these two nations related to Israel that made their refusal to help the Israelites so wrong (cf. Gen. 11:27; 19:36-38)?

    b. There is another reason why Ammon and Moab experienced God's judgment. What is it (Gen. 12:3)?

4. The Ammonites and the Moabites hired a prophet named Balaam to curse Israel when the infant Israelite nation tried to pass through their lands (cf. Nu. 22:7 ff.). Even though Balaam reluctantly agreed to curse Israel, God caused him to bless His people (cf. Nu. 24:3-9). Balaam is a good example of someone who tries to use his spiritual gifts from God for personal benefit rather than for the glory of God.

   a. Every Christian has been given a spiritual gift to be used for God's glory (cf. 1 Cor. 12:7). While some of the spiritual gifts are no longer operational (cf. 1 Cor. 13:8), the proper exercise of spiritual gifts within the church can be a great help to God's work. In what way(s) are you currently using your spiritual gift(s) and abilities for the glory of God?

   b. Some Christians believe that God has given them a spiritual gift for their own personal edification. Why did God give spiritual gifts to the church (1 Cor. 12:7)?

5. Nehemiah was governor of Judah for twelve years (cf. Neh. 2:1, 13:6). During that time, he rebuilt the wall, repopulated Jerusalem, and brought about necessary social and spiritual reform within the Jewish community. Subsequently, he went to Persia for an unspecified period before returning to Jerusalem (Neh. 13:6). Upon his return, Nehemiah found that Eliashib, the high priest in Judah (cf. Neh. 3:1, 20), had prepared a large room for Tobiah, Nehemiah's arch-enemy (Neh. 13:4-7).

   a. How did Nehemiah react to this situation (Neh. 13:8, 9)?

   b. Why was one of the rooms in the temple available for Tobiah to inhabit (Neh. 13:5, 10)?

6. When Nehemiah originally came to Jerusalem, the wall was broken down and the Jewish community was in social and spiritual disarray. God used Nehemiah to restore the wall and the people. However, while he was in Persia the Jews returned to their wicked ways. What important truths do you think this situation teaches us about the work of God?

7. Nehemiah stationed four trustworthy men (a priest, a scribe, a Levite, and a helper) to oversee the distribution of the people's tithes (Neh. 13:13). He also prayed, **Remember me, O my God, concerning this, and do not wipe out my good deeds that I have done for the house of my God, and for its services** (Neh. 13:14). Do you think Nehemiah's prayer was an appeal to God for personal recognition, a request for divine help, or something else?   Why?

8. The Jews obliged themselves in writing to keep the Sabbath (cf. Neh. 10:31), but they forsook their commitment (Neh. 13:15, 16). Some Christians might be tempted to use the Jews' failure as proof of the foolishness of making spiritual commitments. Even though the making of spiritual commitments is endorsed in Scripture (e.g., Jos. 24:15-27), they believe that spiritual commitments are counterproductive, causing Christians to take their eyes off God.

    a. Do you think a Christian should make spiritual commitments?   Why?

    b. Name at least one spiritual commitment you have made since you were saved and explain briefly how this decision has influenced your life.

Study # 7b   **Finishing Your Work**

Read - Neh. 13:1-31; other references as given.

9. Nehemiah admonished some men from Judah for their violation of the Sabbath (Neh. 13:15). He also reprimanded the nobles of Judah by saying, **What evil thing is this that you do, by which you profane the Sabbath day?** (Neh. 13:15-18).

 a. Why do you think Nehemiah did not originally rebuke the men of Tyre (a gentile city northeast of Jerusalem) who were living in the area for importing fish and merchandise and selling them on the Sabbath?

 b. Nehemiah's actions toward the men of Tyre teaches an important spiritual principle regarding the Christian's relationship toward the unsaved. What is it?

10. When Nehemiah rebuked the nobles of Judah for violating the Sabbath, he said they **profaned** it (Heb.-*halal* - to profane or desecrate, to return to common use; Neh. 13:17, 18). What did Nehemiah mean by this (Ex. 20:8-11)?

11. Nehemiah also said, **"Did not your fathers do thus, and did not our God bring all this disaster on us and on this city? Yet you bring added wrath on Israel by profaning the Sabbath."** (Neh. 13:18). To what trouble was Nehemiah referring (Jer. 17:19-27)?

12. Some of those who had been accustomed to trading on the Sabbath spent the night outside the gate (Neh. 13:20). When Nehemiah threatened to use force if they continued to do so, they desisted (v. 21). What else did Nehemiah do to make sure this problem did not continue (Neh. 13:22)?

13. The people of Judah had also promised in writing that they would not intermarry with peoples of the land (i.e., gentile pagans; cf. Neh. 10:30). However, both the lay people and the priests disobeyed God's Law (Neh. 13:23-28). The children who were born to these marriages were not able to speak the language of Judah (i.e., Hebrew, v. 24).

    a. Why did Nehemiah respond so vehemently against these people by cursing them, striking some of them, pulling out their hair, and making them swear to not give their sons and daughters or themselves to intermarriage with gentiles in the future (Neh. 13:25-27)?

    b. Nehemiah prays again for God's remembrance (Neh. 13:29). What does he want God to do this time (v. 29)?

14. What were the most significant spiritual truths that were taught in this study of Nehemiah?

15. a. What spiritual character quality did you observe in Nehemiah's life that you would most like to see developed in your life?

    b. What specific spiritual decisions could you make right now to incorporate the spiritual lessons learned in this study into your life?

Psalm 119:105 "Your word is a lamp to my feet and a light to my path."

Study # 1   The Priority Of Prayer

1.   William Carey.

2.   Nehemiah was a Jewish exile who was born and raised in Persia. His father's name was Hachaliah (Neh. 1:1). He became one of the official cupbearers for King Artaxerxes (Neh. 1:11-2:1). He left the Persian court to help rebuild the wall of Jerusalem so that the Jewish people would be protected from their enemies.

3.   In 586 BC, Nebuchadnezzar and his Babylonian army sacked and burned Jerusalem, bringing an end to the southern kingdom of Judah and their formal occupation of Palestine. Except for the poor of the land, the Jewish people were taken captive to Babylon, as the prophets Isaiah and Jeremiah had prophesied many years earlier.

4.   Cyrus.

5.   a.   Local enemies wrote a letter to King Artaxerxes of Persia accusing the Jews of rebuilding the city so that they could rebel against Persian rule (Ezra 4:11-16). In response to these allegations, King Artaxerxes issued a royal decree that stopped the work until the second year of King Darius of Persia (Ezra 4:24).
     b.   When Ezra arrived at Jerusalem, he found the temple was still not completed and many of the Jews had intermarried with the pagan people of the land. Ezra oversaw the completion of the temple and led the people to renounce their pagan ways.

6.   a.   Nehemiah led the third and final group back to Palestine in 445/444 BC – ninety-four years after Cyrus's original decree.
     b.   During his twelve-year stay in Jerusalem, Nehemiah succeeded in rebuilding the wall surrounding Jerusalem and instituting needed social and religious reforms among the people.

7.   The book of Nehemiah is a sequel to the book of Ezra that provides the final part of the historic record of the Jews' return to Palestine. A second purpose of the book may be to show how mightily God will use someone who is willing to give up his earthly security and trust Him. A third purpose of Nehemiah may be to remind God's people that true spirituality is not the result of proximity to a place of worship. A fourth purpose may be to reveal the level of dedication that is necessary to accomplish great things for God. Nehemiah's opposition came from enemies on both sides of the wall and his perseverance is a testimony to God's faithfulness and his (Nehemiah's) determination.

8. a. 1. Nehemiah asked Hanani about the welfare of the Jewish people who were living in Jerusalem and the surrounding area.
    2. He also asked about the physical condition of the city of Jerusalem.

    b. Hanani told Nehemiah that the people (v. 3, the remnant) were in great distress and reproach. This meant that the Jewish people living in the area were having great difficulty and were at the mercy of their enemies around them. Hanani also said the wall of Jerusalem was broken down and the gates of the city had been burned with fire.

9. Nehemiah was distressed because the city of Jerusalem was desolate and the Jewish people were unprotected (Neh. 2:3). Note: It is likely that Hanani's report of the destruction of Jerusalem (i.e., walls broken down and the gates burned with fire) and Nehemiah's emotional reaction (v. 4) do not refer entirely to the original destruction of the city by Nebuchadnezzar almost 150 years earlier. It is more likely that Nehemiah had expected the city to have been rebuilt by the returning exiles under Zerubbabel and Ezra.

10. a. 1. Jesus met the needs of the multitudes by feeding them (Matt. 14:13-19).
    2. Paul reasoned in the synagogue and in the marketplace every day with those who were present (Acts 17:16, 17).
    3. Epaphroditus - he longed to visit the Philippians and to reassure them that he was healthy (Phil. 2:25-30). Epaphroditus had nearly lost his life as a result of some failure of the Philippians (cf. v. 30).

    b. Christians can show compassion to those in need in the same way as those listed above (part "a"). Like Jesus, God's people can reach out to others with simple hospitality, opening their homes to the unsaved and providing a meal at an appropriate time. Like Paul, they can lovingly explain the scriptures to those who are confused and searching for answers to life. They should do as Paul did, reasoning (not arguing) with those who are being drawn by God (cf. Jn 8:32). Like Epaphroditus, God's people can also visit those in need and reassure them of their love and concern. Other answers could apply.

11. Answers will vary.

12. 1. Adoration - "Lord God of heaven, O great and awesome God" (v. 5).
    2. Confession - "confess the sins of the children of Israel which we have sinned against You; Both my father's house and I have sinned" (v. 6), "We have acted very corruptly against You ..." (v. 7).
    3. Thanksgiving - Nothing specific except he appears to be thankful that God can be expected to be faithful to keep His Word (vv. 8, 9).

4. Supplication - "O Lord, I pray, please let Your ear be attentive to the prayer of Your servant, and to the prayer of Your servants who desire to fear Your name; and let Your servant prosper this day, I pray, and grant him mercy in the sight of this man" (v. 11).

13. a. Your servant(s).
    b. Answers will vary.

14. 1. Nehemiah asked God to fulfill His promise to allow the Jews to return to Palestine if they repented and kept his commandments (vv. 9, 10).
    2. He also asked God to turn the heart of King Artaxerxes (v. 11, "...and let Your servant prosper, this day I pray, and grant him mercy in the sight of this man"). Note: The Persian kings of this historic period had a generous administrative attitude toward the provinces over which they ruled. Nehemiah was probably aware of this benevolent attitude and prayed specifically that the king would act generously on his behalf.

15. a. He prayed a brief prayer and answered the king's question.
    b. Answers will vary.
    c. The love of God being perfected in His people.

16. Nehemiah gave him a definite time. There is an important spiritual principle here: When God directs his people to do a "great work for Him", they need to remember that others might be adversely affected. They should be sensitive to the needs of others around them and do all they can to alleviate any inconveniences or hardships that their decision might cause. A good example of this kind of sensitivity is found in the life of Daniel (cf. Dan. 1:8-16).

17. a. 1. Nehemiah asked King Artaxerxes to give him letters of endorsement to the various governors so that he could pass through the provinces on his way to Jerusalem.
        2. Nehemiah asked the king to give him a letter addressed to Asaph, the keeper of the king's forest, authorizing Asaph to give him all the lumber he needed to rebuild the gates of the fortress, the wall of the city, and a house for himself (Neh. 2:8).
    b. 1. Nehemiah's bold request seems to indicate that he was confident that God was about to answer his prayer (cf. Neh. 1:11, "... let your servant prosper this day, I pray, and grant him mercy in the sight of this man."). When a Christian prays in faith, he should trust God to answer his prayer, stepping out in that confidence.
        2. It also indicates that Nehemiah recognized his responsibility to prepare a detailed plan of how he would accomplish his goal of rebuilding the wall, etc. It is important for God's people to remember that, while they might feel a

strong sense of God's leading regarding a particular matter, others might not always experience the same sense of confidence. A well-prepared plan will help ease the apprehensions of those who will be affected by the believer's decision.

Study # 2   The Power Of A Clear Vision

1.   Two men, Sanballat and Tobiah, were very displeased that Nehemiah had come to seek the welfare of the sons of Israel. Note: These two men were government officials living in the area. Perhaps they saw Nehemiah as a threat to their control of the people.

2.   a. 1.   Nehemiah needed to make a personal assessment of the condition of the wall and formulate a specific plan so that the people would have confidence that he knew what he was doing. If he had revealed an uneducated conceptual plan before surveying the wall, there is little doubt that he would have undermined his credibility. The wall had lain in ruins for approximately 130 years and he needed the wholehearted support of the people to accomplish the task.
        2.   Nehemiah was already aware of resistance to his presence in the area (cf. Neh. 2:10) and he did not need anyone to misrepresent him or his plans' objectives.
     b. 1.   A leader must have a thorough knowledge of the work to be accomplished. Nehemiah did this by inspecting the wall himself. This allowed him to speak with authority and gain the confidence of the people.
        2.   A leader must take care of his physical well-being so that he can effectively meet the challenges ahead. Nehemiah did this by resting three days before he began his work (Neh. 2:11). A leader who is emotionally exhausted is usually ineffective.
        3.   A leader must know how and when to share his goals and objectives. Nehemiah made a thorough examination of the wall, brought the people together, and shared his goal of rebuilding the wall.

3.   1.   He explained the need (i.e., bad situation, reproach) before he shared his vision to rebuild the wall.
     2.   He identified with the people (e.g., "You see the distress that we are in...", "Come and Let us build ...")
     3.   He told the people how God had led him to this point and how King Artaxerxes had endorsed the work.

4.   Answers will vary.

5. a. 1. Nehemiah's enemies attacked his judgment, "What is this thing that you are doing?".
       2. They attacked his motives, "Will you rebel against the king?".
    b. The servant of the Lord must not quarrel but be gentle, able to teach and patient.

6. a. Answers will vary.
    b. Answers will vary but could include the following:
       1. Pray for the wisdom to be more teachable.
       2. Study the Biblical passages that specifically address the characteristics of humility.
       3. Try to accept the criticism of others as a gift from God.
       4. Attempt to focus on the message rather than the manner in which the message was delivered or the messenger who delivers God's message. This will help you overcome the immediate shock of being hurt by the criticism.
       5. Make a conscious decision not to defend yourself when someone criticizes you.

7. "All Scripture is given by inspiration of God, and is profitable for doctrine, for reproof, for correction, for instruction in righteousness, that the man of God may be complete, thoroughly equipped for every good work."

8. It was fitting for the high priest to set an example of supporting the work. If he had been unwilling to contribute, there is little doubt that others would have been reluctant to help (e.g., the Levites, v. 17; the priest, vv. 26, 28). The animals that were brought to the temple for sacrifice were brought in through the Sheep Gate so it was logical that Eliashib should take responsibility for its reconstruction.

9. a. 1. The builders would spend less time traveling to their places of work.
       2. Meals could be brought by family members, thereby saving time and the need for additional workers.
       3. The builders could more easily address family needs during the construction period.
       4. The builders would be motivated to make their portion of the wall secure to discourage an enemy attack at that location.
       5. The builders would be able to help protect their families in the event of an enemy attack.
       6. Other answers could apply.
    b. Answers will vary.

10. 1. The builders would be naturally motivated by the visible progress of the work adjacent to them.
    2. Those builders who worked more slowly would be motivated to increase their productivity by the example of the more efficient workers.
    3. The builders would be able to share building resources and manpower in time of need.
    4. Other answers could apply.

11. a. It appears that Nehemiah did not respond to their unwillingness to help with the work. Even though God had directed Nehemiah to come to Jerusalem and rebuild the wall, all the Jews wholeheartedly supported the work, except this small group of nobles from Tekoa. There is an important spiritual lesson to be learned here. Those who are led by God to do His work must be willing to press forward in the face of external opposition and internal apathy. A wise leader must be able to realize the difference between the necessity of unity and the idealism of unanimity.
    b. The common people from Tekoa, a small town five miles south of Bethlehem.

12. a. Tobiah said the wall would be weak and ineffective even if the builders were able to complete the construction. He did not attack their original plan to rebuild the wall, or their motives. He attempted to undermine their work ethic by indicating that all their labors were going to be in vain.
    b. Nehemiah turned to God in prayer. He acknowledged the viciousness of the attack ("...for we are despised", v. 4) and the effect it had had on the builders (v. 5). He asked God to deal with his enemies by turning their wicked actions on themselves (v. 4) and he asked God to deal with their sin. While Nehemiah's prayer appears to be somewhat unloving (i.e., "Do not cover their iniquity, and do not let their sin be blotted out before from before You ...", v. 5), he was simply asking God in faith to take care of the problem so that they (the builders) could continue to do the work that He had commissioned them to do.

13. a. No. It is very possible that God answered Nehemiah's prayer by directing him to set up the guard day and night. God often answers the believer's prayer by placing practical ideas in his mind that will give him the resolution to the problem. The New Testament writer James said, "If any of you lacks wisdom, let him ask of God, who gives to all liberally ..." (Ja. 1:5).
    b. While God invites His children to come boldly to Him in prayer so that they find mercy and grace (cf. Heb. 2:16), prayer should never be considered an excuse for the believer's personal irresponsibility. The Christian should learn to turn to God in prayer and do the things that God has commanded in His Word.

14. 1.   Nehemiah placed additional men and women and children to protect the lowest parts of the wall (v. 13). If the women and children were the families of the builders who were behind in their work, Nehemiah's action must have been substantial motivation for them to build their portion of the wall.
    2.   Nehemiah called an assembly of the people and told them to focus on the Lord and be ready to fight for their fellow Jews, their families, and their houses (v. 14).

15. a.   God.
    b.   The Jews returned to their work of rebuilding the wall.

16. Nehemiah ordered half the workers to rebuild the wall while the other half protected the people from enemy attack (v. 16). The laborers who could do their work with one hand were told to carry a weapon with the other hand (v. 17). The builders wore a sword at their side (v. 18). Nehemiah also set up a system to rally the people in the event of surprise attack. If there was an attack, the people were to go directly to the place where the trumpet had been blown (v. 20). As they went, they were to remember that God was going to fight for them (v. 20). The builders were to remain inside the wall during the night and stay fully dressed in the event of a night attack (vv. 22, 23).

17. Christians are to protect themselves by putting on the whole armor of God and standing firm in the strength of His might (Eph. 6:10-17). They are to spiritually stand guard over all the saints at all times with prayer (v. 18).

Study # 3   How To Overcome Adversity

1. a.   1.   The poor Jewish families (the people and their wives, v. 1) who faced severe financial hardship due to the reconstruction of the wall and their inability to be gainfully employed during this time.
        2.   The wealthy Jewish people who were exploiting their poor Jewish brothers.
   b.   1.   Some of the Jewish people with large families did not have enough food to eat (v. 2).
        2.   Other poor people had mortgaged their fields, vineyards, and houses to buy food (v. 3).
        3.   Still others had borrowed money to pay the royal tax on their estates (v. 5). In some cases the indebtedness had become so great that the sons and daughters of the people had been sold into slavery. Note: Persia had instituted a tax on the past production of the fields combined with the amount of crops they yielded. This became an excessive burden on the people.

2. a. Nehemiah was very angry.
    b. Nehemiah took some time to evaluate the situation before he confronted the erring Jews. It is likely that he took some time to pray and to consider what God wanted him to do to resolve the problem.

3. Answers will vary.

4. 1. Nehemiah immediately realized the danger of the problem. The morale of the people was already low and the problem might have stopped the construction of the wall. He confronted the problem directly by calling an assembly of the people, including those who had violated God's commandments (v. 7).
    2. He assembled all the people and confronted the wealthy Jews publicly (v. 8). Nehemiah explained how he and others ("we", v. 8) had been doing all they could to redeem Jewish slaves from the surrounding nations (vv. 8, 9).
    3. He challenged the wealthy Jews to stop their sinful conduct and to give back all the property they had taken. He also told them to give back the interest they had charged their fellow Jews (vv. 10, 11). Some scholars believe the hundredth part of the money referred to 1% per month.
    4. He made the Jews vow that they would follow through on their decision to repay the money and to refrain from charging them interest (v. 12).

5. 1. They had charged their fellow Jews interest (usury) on the money they had borrowed which was in direct violation of the Mosaic Law (Ex. 22:25; De. 23:19).
    2. They had exploited their fellow Jews by subjecting them to the humiliation of slavery (Lev. 25:39-43).

6. a. 1. Nehemiah wanted them to stop charging their fellow Jews interest on the money they had borrowed (v. 10).
        2. Nehemiah wanted them to repay all the interest they had charged and to give back any property they had taken (v. 11).
    b. 1. Zacchaeus (Lu. 19:1-8).
        2. Onesimus (Phil. 8-16). Note: Onesimus, a slave, ran away from his owner Philemon. He came in contact with the apostle Paul who led him to Christ. Paul sent Onesimus back to Philemon, encouraging him to receive Onesimus, not as a slave, but as a brother (v. 16). Paul knew that Onesimus needed to go back to clear his conscience and Philemon needed to forgive him before they both could feel right about the situation.
    c. Answers will vary.

7. a. 1. During Nehemiah's twelve-year tenure as governor of Judah, he did not use the governor's daily food allowance even though the previous governors had done so (v. 14).

2.   He did not buy up any land for personal gain but dedicated himself and his servants to the construction of the wall (v. 16).

3.   He supplied food for one hundred and fifty people on a regular basis and an indefinite number of visiting dignitaries at his own expense (v. 17).

b.   1.   Nehemiah had a fear of God that prevented him from taking advantage of the people (v. 15).

2.   Nehemiah knew that the Jewish people were already financially over-burdened (v. 18).

8.   Answers will vary.

9.   He was doing a great work and the work on the wall would stop (v. 3).

10.   Answers will vary. Christians should do everything for the glory of God (1 Cor. 10:31). Everything that a believer does according to God's will should be considered a great work. God's people should attempt to see God's commands for their lives, even the most mundane responsibilities of daily living, from an eternal perspective.

11.   The nature of Sanballat's letter would normally have been considered official government business. The unsealed letter invited the attention and perusal of the courier who likely shared the details of the letter with others - the very thing Sanballat wanted to happen. Sanballat's tactic is similar to Sennacherib's attempt to undermine Hezekiah's leadership by having his ambassadors speak to the Jewish people in Aramiac (cf. 2 Kgs. 18:27-33).

12.   a.   1.   Sanballat did not take credit for the origin of the evil report. He gave credit for the origin of the report to Geshem and general hearsay ("it is reported among the nations", vv.6, 7). Gossips and slanderers are often very careful to protect themselves against future accusations of spreading rumors.

2.   He continued to spread the report rather than checking the authenticity of the information (v. 6). Gossips and slanderers expend their energy spreading their poison rather than verifying the facts.

3.   He assigned sinful motives to Nehemiah's actions rather than going to him directly (vv. 6, 7). Gossips and slanderers are often critical and vengeful people who fail to love others. Rather than bearing all things (the failures of others), believing all things (thinking the best of others rather than the worst), hoping all things (assuming there is a logical answer to the perceived failure or sin) and enduring all things (refusing to spread an evil report), they demonstrate their lack of love for God and the individual by spreading an evil report.

b. Gossip and slander have the power to separate close or intimate friends.

c. A fool.

13. 1. Nehemiah refuted the accusation (v. 8). Although it is generally not wise for a Christian to defend himself against the verbal attacks of ungodly people, there are times when he should refute the false accusation so that his silence is not construed as an admission of guilt (cf. Pro. 26: 5).

2. He turned to God in prayer, asking for strength during this attack (v. 10).

14. a. As a layman, Nehemiah was not permitted to enter the sanctuary (Lev. 21:17-24; Nu. 18:7). In addition, there is a strong possibility that Nehemiah was a eunuch since he served in the Persian court as a cupbearer. If this was so, he would have been forbidden to enter the sanctuary.

b. If Nehemiah had wavered in the face of danger and fled to the sanctuary, his enemies would have been able to discredit his character and successfully undermine the people's confidence in his leadership. This might have been enough to stop the work.

c. Nehemiah turned again to the Lord in prayer.

15. 1. Nehemiah's enemies lost their confidence to continue their attack on him and the people.

2. Nehemiah's enemies realized that the work had been accomplished by the help of God.

16. a. 1. Tobiah's friends spoke well of him to the people of Jerusalem (v. 19).

2. They reported everything Nehemiah did and said to Tobiah (v. 19).

b. Nehemiah probably kept to his work, prayed and did not criticize Tobiah in front of the people.

17. Answers will vary.

Study # 4   One Nation Under God

1. Nehemiah appointed gatekeepers, singers and Levites to serve the people (v. 1). He also appointed Hanani, his brother, and Hananiah, the commander of the fortress, to oversee Jerusalem.

2. a. 1. The Text says that Nehemiah spoke to "them" (v. 3).

2. Jerusalem and the surrounding cities and towns were separated in administrative districts that sometimes included a portion of a city as in the case of Jerusalem (Neh. 3:9, 12).

      b.   He was a faithful man and feared God more than many other men.

3.   a.   1.   God is faithful to not allow believers to be tempted to sin beyond what they are able to bear (1 Cor. 10:13).
          2.   God is faithful to protect believers from the unrestrained power of Satan (2 Thess. 3:3).
          3.   God is faithful to forgive and cleanse believers who come to Him in sincere repentance and confession (1 Jn. 1:9).
   b.   1.   A Christian who is considered faithful must be committed to the Lord.
          2.   A Christian who is faithful must consistently choose to seek the kingdom of God rather than the things of this world (cf. Matt. 6:33).
          3.   A Christian who is faithful must be allowing the Holy Spirit to control his mind and his actions because one of the fruit of the Spirit includes self-control (Gal. 5:23).
          4.   A Christian who is faithful must be absolutely committed to the authority of God's Word, his wife and family, his local church and the ministries that God has given him.
   c.   Answers will vary.

4.   a.   1.   He received his master's commendation ("Well done …").
          2.   He received his master's confidence and was given additional responsibility ("I will make you ruler over many things").
          3.   He received the verbal affirmation that his effort was pleasing to his master ("enter into the joy of your lord").
   b.   If God's people are not faithful to manage the material things that He has entrusted to their care according to His plan, He will not entrust to them the true riches (v. 11).
   b.   The spiritual truths that God is willing to reveal to individuals who are faithful to Him.

5.   1.   There were not many people living in Jerusalem (v. 4). It is likely that Nehemiah wanted to determine the total number of Jews living in Palestine to see if he could convince some of them to move into the city.
      2.   God put the idea in his mind to take a census of the people who had returned from Persia (v. 5).

6.   a.   It appears that Ezra's record may have been taken at the beginning of the return from Persia (cf. Ezra 2:1). The record that Nehemiah found was perhaps the amended final totals of those who actually arrived in Jerusalem. It is not unlikely that such a large group of returning exiles (approx. 42,000), traveling a distance of several hundred miles, would experience substantial changes.
   b.   Some of the priests could not prove their ancestral heritage so they were considered unclean and excluded from the priesthood (v. 64).

7. a. The Law of Moses (i.e., the first five books of the Bible (Genesis – Deuteronomy).
    b. 1. The people were attentive to the reading of the Word (v. 3).
        2. The people stood when Ezra began to read the Word (v. 5).
        3. The people wept when the Word was read to them (v. 9).

8. 1. An unwillingness to read and study the Scriptures on a regular basis.
    2. An unwillingness to obey the commands of Scripture.
    3. An unwillingness to heed the warnings of Scripture.
    4. An unwillingness to witness to the lost of the coming wrath of God. Other answers could apply.

9. a. The Thessalonian believers received God's message spoken through the apostle Paul as the Word of God rather than the words of men.
    b. 1. The Thessalonian believers became imitators of Paul and of the Lord (v. 6).
        2. They accepted the Word joyfully even though they faced persecution ("… in much affliction", v. 6).
        3. They became exemplary spiritual examples to the Christians in the other churches (v. 7).
        4. Their faith in Christ had spread everywhere (v. 8).
        5. They had left their pagan practices of idolatry and began to serve the living and true God (v. 9).
        6. They were anxiously awaiting the return of Jesus Christ (v. 10).
    c. Paul said the Thessalonian believers' witness had been so effective throughout the area that he and his missionary companions had no need to say anything (v. 8).

10. Yes.
    1. It is important for Bible teachers (pastors, evangelists, Sunday School teachers, etc.) to follow the Biblical pattern so that the hearers gain confidence in the authority of God's Word rather than in the speaker's ability to communicate spiritual truth.
    2. It is also important to follow this pattern so that the teacher does not preach his own ideas and opinions instead of the Word of God.
    3. It is important to follow the Biblical pattern so that the teacher does not lead his hearers into a habit of proof-texting. A teacher, who consistently teaches topically and uses the Bible only for proof-texting, will usually find that his hearers develop a habit of using their Bibles in the same way. Rather than studying the context of the passage carefully, they will have a greater tendency to misinterpret the Bible because they often do not study the verses within the specific context in which they were written. Other answers could apply.

11. Paul told Timothy to preach the Word at all times ("be ready in season and out of season", v. 2). Paul told Timothy that there will be times when God's people will not want to hear sound doctrine. They would want to have their ears tickled and they would search out teachers who accommodated their shallow approach to spiritual learning. They would turn away from the truth and turn aside to myths (vv. 3, 4).

12. 1. The traditions of men (Mk. 7:5-9).
     2. Myths and endless genealogies (1 Tim. 3-7).

13. 1. Faith comes from hearing the Word of God (Ro. 10:17).
     2. "All Scripture is given by inspiration of God and is profitable for doctrine, for reproof, for correction, for instruction in righteousness". It is the only means by which a Christian can be thoroughly trained according to the will of God and be equipped to live a godly life (2 Tim. 3:16, 17).
     3. The Word of God is living and active and sharper than a two-edged sword. It has the power to judge the thoughts and motives (intents) of the heart (Heb. 4:12).

14. a. The Jews found out that they should live in booths or temporary dwellings during the Festival of Tabernacles (i.e., booths). This specific religious responsibility had not been done since the days of Joshua (v. 17).
     b. 1. The Jews immediately sent out a proclamation throughout the cities of Judah and Jerusalem, notifying the people of the need to obey the commandment of God (v. 15).
         2. All the people responded to the proclamation by coming to Jerusalem and living in booths (vv. 16, 17).
     c. The Jews rejoiced greatly (v. 17).

15. a. Every Christian father has the spiritual responsibility to not provoke his children to wrath or anger, but to bring them up in the nurture and admonition of the Lord.
     b. 1. He and his wife should pray daily for wisdom to raise their children according to the Word of God.
         2. He should strive to live a dedicated life for God so that his children see a consistent example of spiritual dedication and genuine love for God.
         3. He should love his wife so that the children will honor and obey their mother and listen to her counsel.
         4. He should lead his family in family devotions and prayer so that they see the priority of the Word of God and are trained to duplicate this priority in the next generation.

5. He should become involved in a sound Bible-believing church where the biblical principles he is teaching to his family are reinforced through the teaching ministry of the church and modeled in the lives of the other families. Other answers could apply.

Study # 5   Getting Right With God

1. They fasted while wearing sackcloth and putting dirt on their heads (v. 1). They separated themselves from all foreigners and confessed their sins and the iniquities of their ancestors (v. 2).

2.   a.   1.   Genuine repentance is more than just being sorrowful - it is a change of thinking which is reflected in a change of conduct (v. 9).
           2.   A person who is genuinely repentant understands his error and follows through with the often-embarrassing steps of making things right with those he has wronged (v. 10).
           3.   A person who is genuinely repentant often manifests a serious desire to make things right with those he has wronged ("what diligence", v. 11).
           4.   A person who is genuinely repentant often manifests such a sincere desire to remedy the situation that those offended are convinced that there has been a genuine change of heart ("what clearing of yourselves", v. 11).
           5.   A person who is genuinely repentant often feels indignant over his own spiritual passivity that contributed to his sin ("what indignation", v. 11).
           6.   A person who is genuinely repentant is often fearful that he could duplicate his error at a future time ("what fear", v. 11).
           7.   A person who is genuinely repentant often feels a desire to resolve any personal offenses that may have been caused as a result of his sin ("what vehement desire", v. 11).
           8.   A person who is genuinely repentant often experiences an increased spiritual alertness so that similar problems do not occur in the future ("what zeal", v. 11).
           9.   A person who is genuinely repentant often experiences a willingness to do whatever he has to do to rectify the situation ('what vindication", v. 11). Note: It is interesting to note that, while tears often accompany genuine repentance, they are not an essential characteristic of it.
     b.   A knowledge of genuine repentance can greatly help parents discern whether their children are truly repentant when they have done wrong. If a parent does not know the Biblical characteristics of genuine repentance, he can be deceived by false expressions of repentance (e.g., tears, promises to obey in the future, insincere apologies, etc.) even though the child has not come to genuine repentance. This can encourage a child to develop a host of psychological tools

to appease others rather than coming to true repentance. If this happens the child will soon develop a guilty conscience and other problems.

3. The Jewish leaders realized that Israel's dismal spiritual history and present political situation (i.e., slavery) were a result of the nation's failure to fulfill the conditions of the covenant. God viewed the nation as a single entity and foreigners were not part of the original problem that resulted in their servitude or part of the solution that might remedy the situation.

4.   a.   God's name is weighty because His name is a reflection of His character. Everything God says (His commandments, promises, warnings, etc.) should be taken carefully, seriously and everything He does should be evaluated closely.

    b.   The covenant that God established with Abraham made specific provisions for his descendants to give them the land of promise (Gen. 15:18-21). The Jews of Nehemiah's day realized that their present condition (i.e., slavery) was a direct result of disobedience to God's Word.

5.   a.   1.   The Levites praised God that He alone is the Lord (v. 6).
        2.   They praised God for His creative work (v. 6).
        3.   They praised God for giving life (v. 6).
        4.   They praised God for choosing Abraham, bringing him out of Ur of the Chaldees and making a covenant with him (v. 7).
        5.   They praised God for fulfilling His word to Abraham (v. 8).

    b.   Answers will vary.

6.   a.   1.   God saw their affliction (v. 9).
        2.   He heard their cry by the Red Sea (v. 9).
        3.   He delivered His people from the hand of Pharaoh ("showed signs and wonders against Pharaoh") by dividing the Red Sea ... (v. 10).

    b.   As part of the Abrahamic Covenant the Lord promised to judge those who fought against His people (Gen. 12:3).

7.   a.   Just, true, and good.
    b.   1.   They acted proudly, hardened their hearts, and would not heed to God's commandments (vv. 16, 17).
        2.   They forgot all the wondrous deeds God had performed for them (v. 17).
        3.   They appointed a leader to help them return to Egypt (v. 17).

8. Like the ancient Israelites, they begin to act proudly, to refuse to listen to God's commandments, and to forget the wondrous deeds that God has performed for them (vv. 16, 17). They also soon find themselves on their way back into the world (e.g., Egypt, v. 17).

9. 1. God did not forsake them (v. 19).
    2. He continues to guide them by a cloud by day and a pillar of fire by night (v. 19).
    3. God gave them the Holy Spirit (good spirit) to guide them (v. 20).
    4. God fed them with manna and gave them water to drink in their wilderness wanderings (v. 20).
    5. God met their every need down to the most minute detail such as not allowing their clothes to wear out and their feet to swell (v. 21).

10. a. 1. Moses commanded the Israelites to obey all the commandments that God had given them at Mount Sinai (De. 8:1).
        2. He told them to remember how God had led them in the wilderness (v. 2).
        3. He told them not to forget the Lord God when they entered the Promised Land (v. 11).
        4. He told them not to let their hearts become proud.
    b. 1. The Israelites became disobedient and rebelled against God.
        2. They disregarded the commandments of God ("cast Your law behind their backs").
        3. They killed the prophets who reminded them of their error.
        4. They committed great blasphemies.

11. The Old Testament judges who ruled over Israel after Moses, Joshua, and the elders but before Israel's first king, Saul (ca. 1400-1050 BC).

12. 1. The Jews returned to their sin and soon found themselves under enemy oppression again (v. 28).
    2. Many times God delivered the Israelites when they cried to Him for deliverance (v. 28).
    3. God admonished them through the prophets to obey His commands and receive the covenant blessings but they refused to listen (v. 29).
    4. God bore with them for many years even though they refused to listen (v. 30).
    5. When the people refused to listen, God delivered them over to neighboring heathen nations so that they would be oppressed and return to Him.

13. Some of the Jewish leaders, Levites, and priests signed and sealed a written agreement that stated they would commit themselves to follow God.

14. a.   Answers will vary.
    b.   Answers will vary but could include the following:
         1.   Parents should make a commitment to grow in Christ and to be all they can for God.
         2.   Parents should become actively involved in a Bible-believing church where they can be instructed from God's Word and serve others.
         3.   Parents should seek to understand the weaknesses and failures of their parents and to make a concerted effort to overcome these genealogical weaknesses by the grace of God.

15. 1.   They made a commitment to avoid intermarriages with non-Jews (Neh. 10:30; cf. Ex. 34:16; De. 7:3, 4).
    2.   They made a commitment to keep the Sabbath and the sabbatical year (Neh. 10:31; De. 15:1-3).
    3.   They made a commitment to support the temple service (Neh. 10:32, 33).
    4.   They made a commitment to bring their tithes to the Levites for support of those serving the temple (vv. 35-39).

16. 1.   Christians should make a commitment to not marry non-Christians (cf. 2 Cor. 6:14-16).
    2.   Christians should set aside one day a week for spiritual renewal in which they meet together with other believers for worship and instruction. The writer of Hebrews exhorts God's people to increase their fellowship with other Christians as the return of Christ comes closer (cf. Heb. 10:25).
    3.   Christians should financially support the work of the Lord through their local church.
    4.   Christians should give generously and consistently to the work of the Lord for the support of pastors and missionaries who have given their lives for the spiritual advancement of God's people.

17. a.   In the specific context it means more than simply participating in regular corporate worship. Included was the support of the work of the Lord as prescribed in the Law of Moses.
    b.   Answers will vary.

Study # 6   Celebrating God's Victories

1.   The Jews who were living outside of Jerusalem cast lots to identify those who would move into the city. Those who were chosen relocated to Jerusalem to help repopulate the city.

2.   No. The casting of lots was used by the Jews during the Old Testament period (Lev. 16:9, 10; Jos. 21:4, 5; Pro. 16:33. etc.) until the beginning of the New Testament period. The Bible does not mention the use of the lot after the selection of Matthias, the disciple who replaced Judas (cf. Acts 1:26). The New Testament provides clear instruction to Christians how they can determine God's will for their lives.

3.   a.   Answers will vary.
     b.   A Christian must do three things before he is able to consistently discern God's will for his life. 1. He must totally dedicate himself to God ("present your bodies a living sacrifice ...", v. 1). 2. He must separate himself from all worldly actions and attitudes ("be not conformed to this world", v. 2). 3. He must allow his mind to be constantly transformed by the word of God ("be transformed by the renewing of your mind", v. 2). To the extent that the Christian has done these things, he will be able to prove or discern (Gr. *dokimadzo* - to test, to approve, to recognize as genuine after careful examination) God's will.

4.   a.   The people blessed all the men who volunteered to move to Jerusalem.
     b.   Answers will vary.
     c.   Volunteerism inspires other believers to manifest a servant's heart as well (cf. Mk. 10:42-45). Other answers could apply.
     d.   Answers will vary.

5.   a.   1.   Many successive priests were needed due to attrition resulting from death (Heb. 7:23, 24).
          2.   It indicates the weakness of the men who served in that capacity (Heb. 7:28).
          3.   It indicates that the Old Testament sacrifices was never able to permanently absolve the individual's payment for sin (Heb. 10:11).
     b.   Jesus Christ, the Son of God.

6.   1.   The Law was not given to provide mankind with salvation (Ro. 3:19, 20; 8:1-3).
     2.   The Law does not provide God's people with a means of sanctification (i.e., the means by which God's people grow in Christ; Ga. 4:9-11).

7. 1. An effective leader assumes the responsibility of administrative oversight
        of those who are responsible to him (v. 9).
    2. An effective overseer leads those who are assigned to him rather than
        driving or following his people (vv. 11, 17).
    3. An effective leader must assume responsibility for the work assigned to him ("had
        the oversight", vv. 16, 21). He cannot blame someone else for the group's
        inability to accomplish their assignment. Other answers could apply.

8. a. 1. He is not receptive to the proclamation of the Word (v. 9).
        2. He has a critical attitude toward the spiritual leadership that God has
            placed over him ("prating against us", v. 10).
        3. He is verbally critical of spiritual leaders, even to the point of making
            unjustifiable accusations against them ("prating against us with malicious
            words", v. 10).
        4. He is divisive within the church ("he himself does not receive the brethren",
            v. 10).
        5. He adopts an arrogant attitude toward other people in the church and tries to
            exert authority over them (v. 10).
    b. Answers will vary.

9. 1. Music should express thanksgiving to God.
    2. Music should be a sincere expression of our love for God rather than simply a
        presentation of musical talent.
    3. Music (i.e., the lyrics) should have a remedial (teaching) aspect to them that
        instructs and challenges the hearers to live for God.

10. It is important to remember that God's Word is His inspired revelation to man for all
    ages and all peoples. The genealogical records listed throughout Scripture provide
    God's people with the history of man's existence and a vivid reminder of human frailty.
    The genealogical records, with their ever-present reminder of the brevity of life, help
    believers realize that life is not to be squandered. Other answers could apply.

11. 1. They sought out the Levites in the towns and had them come to Jerusalem (vv.
        27-29).
    2. The priests purified themselves, the people, the gates, and the wall (v. 30).
    3. The leaders of the community were brought up on the top of the wall (v. 31).
    4. Two great choirs were organized and began to move in opposite directions
        around the wall (v. 31).

12. a. Answers will vary.

    b. Recommendations/suggestions - A Christian should prepare himself physically, spiritually and emotionally to worship the Lord every Sunday. He can do this by not being out late on Saturday night so he is prepared to worship God. He should plan to get to church early so that he feels relaxed and prepared to worship. He should pray for the service, the message, and for his own receptivity to the spiritual truths that he will hear. He should seek to sing the congregational songs from his heart, thinking about the message of each song. He should desire to minister to others before and after the church service, seeking to some special need within the church body. If the Christian is a father of small children, it would be a good idea to have the children's clothes prepared and set out on Saturday night and their Bibles located and placed in a convenient place. The children should be served a nutritious breakfast that will sustain them until after the service. The parents should teach their children the importance of worshipping God with other believers. Other answers could apply.

13. 1. The two great choirs (companies), Nehemiah, half of the officials and several priests took their stand together in the house of the Lord (vv. 40-42).

    2. The singers sang, offered great sacrifices, and rejoiced so loudly that the noise could be heard from afar (v. 43).

14. a. They sang and offered sacrifices to the Lord in accordance with the Lord's commands. As a result God gave them joy as He will all those who walk in His ways with a humble heart.

    b. If a Christian dedicates himself to fulfilling the will of God as revealed in His Word, God will give the individual joy (Jn. 15:11, 17:13).

    c. Answers will vary.

Study # 7   Finishing Your Work

1. The Jews discovered that the Ammonites and Moabites were not allowed to enter the assembly of God.

2. a. The Jews excluded all foreigners (i.e., the Ammonites and the Moabites) from Israel.

    b. When Israel left Egypt under Moses' leadership, the Ammonites and the Moabites did not assist Israelites as they sought to pass through their land (Neh. 13:2). They hired Balaam, a prophet of God, to curse the Israelites (Nu. 22:1-6). They also prepared themselves for battle against God's people. As a result, God judged these two nations (according to His promise within the Abrahamic Covenant; cf. Gen. 12:3) for attempting to fight against His people.

3. a. Abraham, the patriarch of the Jewish people, was the uncle of Lot (Gen. 11:27). When the Lord destroyed Sodom and Gomorrah, Lot and his family were rescued. Lot's two daughters, fearing that they would be childless, deceived their father and engaged in illicit sex with him (Gen. 19:30-32). The two sons who were born as a result of these incestuous engagements, Moab and Ben-Ammi, became the patriarchs of the Moabite and Ammonite nations (Gen. 19:36-38).
    b. The Moabites and Ammonites attempted to curse God's people which made God curse them (Gen. 12:3).

4. a. Answers will vary.
    b. God has given spiritual gifts to believers for the common good. This means that spiritual gifts are given for the spiritual benefit of the body of Christ - not for the self-glorification of the individual believer, as was the case in the Corinthian church.

5. a. 1. Nehemiah threw all of Tobiah's household goods out of the room (v. 8).
        2. He ordered the rooms to be cleansed (v. 9).
        3. He had the utensils, grain offering, and the frankincense returned to the house of God (v. 9).
    b. The people had failed again to support the Levites and the temple singers with their tithes and offerings (vv. 5, 10). The Levites had returned to their own farms, leaving the administration of the temple services to those who stayed behind.

6. 1. There is a tendency among God's people to gravitate toward secularization.
    2. Christians must be aware of this subtle slide toward secularization and be alert to their own need for spiritual renewal.
    3. God's people must make spiritual commitments that will remind them of their need to walk according to His plan. If they do not, their spiritual condition will continue to deteriorate (Note: this principle might be aptly called the law of "spiritual entropy").
    4. God often uses man (in this case, only one man) to bring about spiritual restoration and renewal among His people.
    5. The construction of religious landmarks (e.g., the wall around Jerusalem, modern church buildings, etc.) will not guarantee spiritual vitality among God's people. Other answers could apply.

7. A request for divine help. Nehemiah has demonstrated little regard for personal advancement (cf. Neh. 1:3-11, 2:4-20, 5:14-19). Nehemiah was likely asking God to bless his efforts for spiritual reform and to not bring additional judgment upon the Israelites for their sins.

8. a. Yes.
   1. Biblical history reveals the inability of God's people to avoid secularization without spiritual commitments.
   2. The making of spiritual commitments is solidly supported in Scripture (cf. Jos. 24:15-27; Jn. 21:15-19; Ro. 12:1, 2, etc.). Note: it is important to note that making of spiritual commitments will not guarantee continuing spiritual vitality. The believer must remember that the spiritual commitments he has made are simply a reminder of his crippling spiritual weakness and his continuing need for God's grace. A spiritual commitment must lead God's people to Him rather than away from Him. Other answers could apply.
   b. Answers will vary.

9. a. As Gentiles they were not under the Law of Moses.
   b. God's people must not expect the unsaved to live according to His plan. While it is true that all men have a conscience and bear the image of God within them (cf. Ro. 2:14-16), they are still natural men who are blinded by Satan (cf. 1 Cor. 2:14, 2 Cor. 4:4). They do not possess the power of the Holy Spirit to overcome the world, the devil, and the flesh. Note: While the actions of the unsaved are often offensive to believers, believers should realize that their greatest desire should be to see the unsaved come to Christ, rather than simply seeing them become more "christianized".

10. God set the seventh day (i.e., the Sabbath) apart for His use and the spiritual benefit of His people (Ex. 20:8-11). By setting it apart, He made it holy, which means that the day was no longer available for common use. The Sabbath day was not to be used by His people for secular purposes (i.e., routine business). When the Jews engaged in regular business of the Sabbath, they were profaning that which God had separated for holy purposes. The Jews were not trusting God to provide for them during the other six days of the week and they were not separating themselves weekly for a time of spiritual renewal.

11. Nehemiah was referring to the original violation of the Law of Moses that caused the nation of Judah to be taken into captivity by Babylon (Jer. 17:19-27). Nehemiah told the Jews that they had fallen prey to the same error as their fathers. He also said God would not look at their sin as an isolated transgression but as part of Israel's continuing rebellion against Him (adding to the wrath on Israel, v. 18).

12. 1. Nehemiah asked the Levites to help the gatekeepers remember that the Sabbath day was holy.
    2. Nehemiah asked God to show mercy (Heb. *hesed* - loyal love) and to honor his willingness to be faithful to His will.

13. a.   While Nehemiah's actions may seem inappropriate for a man of God, he realized that God would not tolerate their sin. He realized that this violation of the Mosaic covenant would bring God's judgment and he wanted to express his complete disgust for their wickedness. The pulling out of a Jewish man's beard was an act of humiliation and Nehemiah wanted to help the Jews realize their need to be humbled before God. Solomon had been lead into idolatry by the very same sin.

   b.   Nehemiah prayed that God would judge those who had intermarried with the peoples of the land rather than judge the entire nation.

14. Answers will vary.

15. a.   Answers will vary.
   b.   Answers will vary.